Practitioner To Icon

Practitioner To Icon

Deepti Gupta

Worldwide Published by
Pendown Press

PENDOWN PRESS LLP

An ISO 9001 & ISO 14001 Certified Co.,

Regd. Office: 3767A, Kanhaiya Nagar,
Tri Nagar, Delhi-110035

Ph.: 8130886000, 9650072927, 8595249536

E-mail: info@pendownpress.com

Branch Office: 1A/2A, 20, Hari Sadan, Ansari Road,
Daryaganj, New Delhi-110002

Ph.: 011-45794768

Website: PendownPress.com

Edition: 2024

Price: ₹ 599

ISBN: 978-93-6338-027-1

Layout and Cover Designed by Pendown Graphics Team
Printed and Bound in India by Thomson Press India Ltd.

Dedicated To My Parents, Who Taught Me The Value Of Compassion, Hard Work, And Kindness. Your Influence Has Shaped Me Into The Person I Am Today.

CONTENTS

Are you ready to elevate your medical practice and transform your career?

Doesn't matter whether you're starting your medical career or you're a seasoned specialist- this Book is perfect for you!

After reading this book you will get 360° clarity on:

- ➢ How to attract the right patients?
- ➢ Building lasting trust with patients.
- ➢ Ensuring a steady flow of patient inquiries.

Plus, you'll discover the secrets to increasing patient engagement, boosting your online reputation, and growing a thriving medical practice that makes a real difference in the lives of your patients.

Let's grow together in the world of medicine.

-Deepti Gupta

Context

So, why are some medical practices thriving while others are merely surviving?

Playing it safe is a dying strategy.

I firmly believe that if you are not learning, you are dying!

A wise man learns from his mistakes, while a genius learns from other people's mistakes.

- Completely revolutionize your medical practice
- Gain cutting-edge patient-attraction strategies that work NOW, so you're not left behind
- Enjoy double-digit growth regardless of competition, taxation changes, and other factors outside of your control

Preface

The healthcare industry is undergoing a transformative shift. What was once a predominantly clinical field is now a complex interplay of medicine, business, and technology. This book is your guide to navigating this new landscape. It's a blueprint for medical professionals seeking to not just survive, but thrive in a competitive market.

Imagine a world where your clinic is always full, patients love you, and your work is less stressful. Sounds good, right? That's what this book is all about. We'll show you how to make your clinic shine, attract new patients, and keep the ones you have happy.

Within these pages, you'll discover strategies to enhance your practice's visibility, build a loyal patient base, and optimize operational efficiency. From mastering the digital realm to cultivating a high-performing team, this book offers practical insights and actionable advice.

From understanding online stuff to building a great team, we've got you covered everything. Let's work together to make your clinic the best it can be.

Are you ready to redefine your practice? Let's rewrite the rules of healthcare together.

Introduction

But first things first, who am I, and what do I know about the Medical Business?

Hello, my name is Deepti Gupta, and I am the Growth Catalyst & Marketing Strategist for hungry and passionate medical practitioners. My journey of coaching doctors to grow their medical practices began seven years ago, late in my career. Prior to that, I spent 15 years working as a Senior Business Strategist with corporates. Since then, I've been continuously impressed, not only by establishing lasting relationships with my clients but also by generating patients for my business.

I live and breathe marketing & coaching doctors daily, and it continues to top my list. Over these years, I have successfully used these marketing strategies and techniques to build my own business and helped numerous small medical practitioners, nursing home owners, doctors who are starting their medical practices, and corporates get more from these marketing strategies.

Acknowledgments

I was always passionate about empowering doctors, who have the potential to make a significant impact on countless lives, and had a mission to share my knowledge with the community. I am humbled and grateful to acknowledge the support and guidance that has made this book possible.

First and foremost, I extend my heartfelt gratitude to Dr. Amit Gupta, whose expertise and mentorship have been invaluable to me. Your guidance and belief in me have been a constant source of inspiration.

To my loving family, who have supported me unconditionally, thank you for your unwavering belief in me and constant encouragement. Your love and sacrifices have enabled me to pursue my dreams.

I am also deeply thankful to my mentor, Shri Akshar Yadav, whose constant motivation and guidance helped me write this book, which can help humanity in multiple ways.

To my dear friends, who have been my pillars of strength, thank you for your support, encouragement, and valuable feedback. Your presence in my life has made a significant difference.

Thank you all again for your support, guidance, and love. I am grateful for your presence in my life.

Why This Book?

You might be wondering why I am sharing this FREE e-book when I could charge a premium for sharing the information. After all, if you implement the suggestions contained within this e-book you can make a real killing and grow your medical practice in leaps & bounds. Besides, as we often learn in the business parlance, “there is no free lunch,“ so why this free e-book?

Being in love with the medical fraternity, I have seen all the pain doctors go through, and it breaks my heart to see how this intelligent breed of humanity is being mistreated and misunderstood by patients. Moreover, most of the doctors stagnate and have limited vision. Thus, I aim to put as many doctors as possible on the right path.

Secondly, I am unable to coach everyone personally due to time constraints, so this e-book is my gift to budding doctors and hospital owners, sharing valuable lessons I have learned during my journey as a successful marketing strategist. I hope these lessons will guide you on the path to success with these marketing strategies.

So, without further ado, let's explore the hidden strategies I've learned.

❍ ❍ ❍ ❍

CHAPTER 1

Why Do Doctors Need Marketing in This New Era?

In this era of rapid technological advancement and heightened competition, the need for doctors to embrace marketing strategies has become paramount. The traditional perception of healthcare as a solely selfless profession is evolving, and doctors are realizing the importance of establishing a strong online presence and brand identity.

With patients increasingly relying on the Internet for healthcare information, a well-executed marketing strategy can help doctors reach a wider audience.

Moreover, the healthcare landscape has become more consumer-centric, with patients actively seeking out medical services that align with their preferences and values.

Effective marketing allows doctors to showcase their expertise, specialties, and patient-centered approach, fostering trust and connection with potential patients. Social media platforms provide a powerful medium for doctors to engage with their community, share valuable health information, and build relationships beyond the confines of the clinic.

Furthermore, marketing is essential for doctors to stay competitive in today's saturated healthcare market. It enables them to differentiate themselves, highlight unique services, and attract a diverse patient base.

As patients become increasingly discerning consumers of healthcare services, doctors who embrace marketing not only enhance their visibility but also contribute to the overall improvement of healthcare accessibility and information dissemination in this era.

Now, the main thing is: I will be making marketing simple for you. Save your money and your time by following a very simple checklist for all social media platforms.

The main idea is to do it yourself instead of relying on any third party. I strongly believe that nobody can work as hard for your business as you will. So, why give away the control of marketing and getting more customers for your business to anyone else? Save money by following these tried-and-tested frameworks. Follow the tips and tricks that I have laid out for you in this module to optimize your marketing budget and get the most out of every penny spent!

Overview of Marketing & Why is it Important?

Marketing is the process of promoting products or services to potential customers. It's crucial for businesses as it helps attract new customers, retain existing ones, and drive revenue growth. By understanding customer needs, building brand awareness, and engaging with audiences effectively, marketing enables businesses to succeed in competitive markets and achieve their goals.

Marketing for doctors is the means through which one can help others by spreading the right education and awareness. If you are doing your marketing, that means you are helping more patients with your services and knowledge. And money is the outcome. However, money cannot be the primary aim. You need to create the real reason.

Here are some tips and tricks to optimize your marketing budget and maximize its effectiveness:

- **Understanding Patient Needs:** Doctors need to understand the healthcare needs and preferences of their target patient demographics. This involves conducting patient surveys, analyzing medical trends, and staying informed about local healthcare challenges and opportunities.
- **Building Trust and Credibility:** Patients seek medical professionals they can trust. Doctors should focus on building credibility through transparent communication, patient testimonials, and sharing relevant medical expertise through blog posts, articles, or seminars.
- **Utilizing Patient Referrals:** Word-of-mouth remains a powerful marketing tool in healthcare. Doctors can encourage satisfied patients to refer their friends and family by providing exceptional care and service.

Offering referral incentives or discounts can also incentivize patients to recommend the practice.

- **Online Presence and Reputation Management:** Maintaining a strong online presence is crucial for doctors in today's digital age. This includes having a professional website, active social media profiles, and positive reviews on healthcare directories. Responding promptly to patient inquiries and feedback demonstrates attentiveness and care.
- **Educational Content Creation:** Doctors can create educational content to engage with patients and address common health concerns or questions. This content can take various forms, such as informative blog posts, instructional videos, or live Q&A sessions on social media platforms. Providing valuable information establishes the doctor as a trusted authority in their field.
- **Targeted Advertising:** Doctors can use targeted advertising strategies to reach specific patient demographics or promote specialized services. For example, advertising campaigns can be tailored to target individuals within a certain geographic area or age group who may benefit from preventive screenings or specialized treatments.
- **Community Involvement:** Participating in community events, health fairs, or local charity initiatives allows doctors to connect with residents and raise awareness about their practice. By demonstrating a commitment

to community health and well-being, doctors can foster positive relationships and attract new patients.

- **Patient-Centered Communication:** Effective communication is essential in healthcare marketing. Doctors should focus on delivering personalized, empathetic care and actively listening to patients' concerns. Clear communication about treatment options, medical procedures, and follow-up care helps build trust and confidence in the doctor-patient relationship.
- **Measuring Results and Adjusting Strategies:** Doctors should track key performance indicators (KPIs) such as patient inquiries, appointment bookings, and patient satisfaction scores to evaluate the effectiveness of their marketing efforts. Analyzing data allows doctors to identify areas for improvement and adjust their strategies accordingly.
- **Compliance with Healthcare Regulations:** It's essential for doctors to ensure that their marketing efforts comply with healthcare regulations and ethical guidelines. This includes protecting patient privacy and confidentiality, obtaining consent for marketing communications, and avoiding misleading or deceptive advertising practices.

By implementing these strategies, doctors can optimize their marketing efforts to attract new patients, retain existing ones, and build a reputable practice in their community.

Now, here is a question for you: What do you understand about marketing?

Hidden Strategy No. 1: Take Great Care of Your Best Patients Who Trust You (Because If You Don't, Someone Else Will!)

In a world of competition, taking great care of your best patients isn't just good practice, it's a hidden strategy for success. These patients, the ones who trust you implicitly, have the potential to become your most vocal advocates.

Imagine your best patients as more than just customers — envision them as loyal fans, or even a "tribe" as Seth Godin describes [Seth Godin Tribes book]. By making them feel special and valued members of your inner circle, you foster an unbreakable bond.

The point is you want them to feel very special because they are part of your inner circle.

The Key Point: What Does it Take to Be the Patient's First Choice?

Becoming the Patient's Go-To Choice

So, how do you secure the coveted position of being a patient's first choice? Here are a few tips:

- **Exceptional Care:** This goes without saying, but provide the highest quality care possible. Address their needs thoroughly, listen attentively, and prioritize their well-being.

- **Personalized Touch:** Remember their preferences, medical history, and even small details. A thoughtful gesture goes a long way.
- **Proactive Communication:** Keep them informed and involved in their healthcare journey. Update them on test results, answer questions promptly, and be easily accessible.
- **Go the Extra Mile:** Small gestures like sending a birthday card or offering extended appointment hours can make a big difference.
- **Show Gratitude:** Thank them for their trust and loyalty. A handwritten note or a simple "thank you" expresses your appreciation.

By implementing these strategies, you'll cultivate a loyal following of patients who will not only return to you but also enthusiastically recommend you to their network. Remember, happy patients are your best marketers!

❍ ❍ ❍ ❍

CHAPTER 2

Increase Your Authority and Credibility

Establishing credibility and authority in the medical field is crucial for gaining the trust of patients and peers alike. By adopting strategic approaches, healthcare professionals can significantly enhance their standing and influence within the industry. Here are ten key strategies to consider:

- **Continuous Education and Specialization:** Stay updated with the latest medical advancements through continuous education and consider specializing in a particular field. Certifications and additional qualifications can enhance credibility.
- **Publish Research and Articles:** Contribute to medical literature by publishing research findings, articles, or case studies. This not only adds to the body of knowledge but also establishes you as an authority in your field.
- **Active Involvement in Medical Associations:** Join and actively participate in medical associations and societies related to your specialty. Attend conferences,

present research, and engage in discussions to build professional relationships and credibility.

- **Online Presence and Thought Leadership:** Develop a strong online presence through a professional website and active engagement on social media. Share valuable medical insights, participate in healthcare discussions, and establish yourself as a thought leader in your field.
- **Patient Testimonials and Reviews:** Encourage satisfied patients to provide testimonials and positive reviews. Positive feedback from patients can significantly boost credibility and attract new patients.
- **Collaboration with Peers:** Collaborate with other healthcare professionals, both within and outside your specialty. Building partnerships and participating in collaborative efforts can enhance your professional network and credibility.
- **Community Involvement:** Actively engage in community health initiatives, workshops, and awareness programs. Demonstrating a commitment to community health can enhance your reputation and credibility among local residents.
- **Effective Communication Skills:** Develop strong communication skills both in written and verbal forms. Clearly explaining medical concepts to patients, colleagues, and the public can enhance your authority and trustworthiness.

- **Ethical and Compassionate Practice:** Uphold the highest ethical standards and prioritize compassionate patient care. Patients are more likely to trust and respect a healthcare professional who demonstrates integrity and empathy.
- **Media Appearances and Public Speaking:** Consider opportunities for media appearances or public speaking engagements. Sharing your expertise on relevant health topics in public forums can significantly elevate your credibility.

By incorporating these strategies into your medical practice, you can enhance your credibility and authority, gaining the trust of both patients and peers in the ever-evolving landscape of healthcare.

Hidden Strategy No. 2: Increase Your Authority and Credibility

In today's information age, establishing yourself as a credible authority figure is a powerful strategy to attract new patients. Don't be afraid to showcase your expertise — it's time to "shout from the rooftops" (figuratively speaking)!

Rise Above the Competition

Simply being a good doctor isn't enough anymore. Go the extra mile and actively distinguish yourself from your competitors. Here's how:

- **Become a Thought Leader:** Share your knowledge and insights with the community. Give lectures, write articles for local publications, or even create informative content for social media.
- **Publish Your Expertise:** Consider authoring a book in your field. A published work acts as a prestigious calling card, solidifying your expertise and attracting patients seeking a trusted authority.
- **Embrace Public Speaking:** Offer to speak at community events or patient education seminars. This allows you to connect with a wider audience and showcase your knowledge.

The Key: Communicate Your Mission, Character, and Code of Conduct

Beyond showcasing your skills, establish your core values and principles.

What drives you as a doctor?

What sets your practice apart?

Clearly communicate your mission statement, guiding philosophy, and approach to patient care. This transparency fosters trust and allows patients to identify with your vision.

By implementing these strategies, you'll position yourself as a trusted authority in your field. Patients will be drawn to your expertise and the clear values you represent.

CHAPTER 3

Build an Iconic Brand: "YOU" be "YOUR" Own Brand?

In the dynamic realm of healthcare, establishing oneself as a brand is a powerful strategy for doctors seeking recognition and trust. Here's a guide on how doctors can craft and amplify their personal brand:

- **Define Your Unique Value Proposition (UVP):** Identify what sets you apart. Whether it's a specialized skill, a unique approach to patient care, or a commitment to innovation, clarify what makes your practice distinctive.
- **Craft a Compelling Narrative:** Develop a personal story that resonates with your audience. Share your journey, challenges, and motivations. A compelling narrative helps humanize your brand, fostering a deeper connection with patients.
- **Professional Online Presence:** Create a polished and professional online presence. This includes a well-designed website, active social media profiles, and

professional headshots. Consistent branding across platforms reinforces your image and makes you easily recognizable.

- **Engage in Thought Leadership:** Share your expertise through blogs, articles, or social media posts. Establish yourself as a thought leader by contributing valuable insights to relevant healthcare discussions. This not only enhances your credibility but also amplifies your brand.
- **Patient-Centric Approach:** Prioritize patient satisfaction and care. Positive patient experiences contribute significantly to your brand reputation. Encourage patient testimonials and leverage them to showcase the human side of your practice.
- **Networking and Collaborations:** Build a strong professional network by collaborating with other healthcare professionals. Partnerships can extend your reach and reinforce your brand through shared expertise and resources.
- **Educational Initiatives:** Offer educational content to your audience. This can include informational videos, webinars, or written materials. Providing valuable information positions you as an authority in your field, strengthening your brand presence.
- **Consistent Branding Elements:** Utilize consistent branding elements, such as a logo or a tagline, across various platforms. Consistency fosters brand

recognition, making it easier for patients to remember and refer to you.

- **Feedback and Adaptation:** Solicit feedback from patients and peers to continually refine your brand. Adapt to evolving trends and healthcare needs, ensuring your brand remains relevant and responsive.
- **Community Engagement:** Participate in community events, health fairs, or charitable initiatives. Active involvement in the community strengthens your local brand presence and fosters a positive perception among residents.

In the era of individualized healthcare experiences, doctors can transform themselves into recognizable and trusted brands by strategically blending personal and professional elements. By following these steps, physicians can cultivate a distinct brand identity that resonates with patients and peers alike.

Hidden Strategy No. 3: Build an Ionic Brand

Branding is the promise you make and the promise that you keep.

- **Finding Your "Why":** Before you start, it is best to get a better understanding of why you are in business for yourself. Very few doctors really understand the 'why', which is a pity because the 'why' is where the power is.
- **Understanding Your Patients:** Building a brand that resonates requires a deep understanding of your

patients. What are their needs, anxieties, and desired outcomes? Look beyond the medical aspect and consider the emotional impact of their experience.

- **The Power of Positioning:** This patient-centric approach forms the basis of powerful positioning. By understanding your ideal patient and crafting a brand that speaks directly to their needs, you set yourself apart and pave the way for an iconic brand.
- **Serving, Not Selling:** Iconic brands prioritize serving their customers. Focus on how you can truly improve your patients' lives, not just on selling them services.
- **Protect Your Brand at All Costs:** Remember that in life, all you have is your name, reputation, and credibility, and if you don't protect them, they will wash away.

What Should You Do?

- Buy a domain for a review site and get testimonials from as many patients as possible. Then spread them out among all your websites.
- Respond to both positive and negative reviews promptly and professionally. Thank satisfied patients and acknowledge concerns raised in negative reviews.
- Use a free WordPress blog; it will maximize your SEO.
- If you are receiving many negative reviews, then you need to take a good, hard look at your business and perhaps get legal or PR experts involved.

CHAPTER 4

Create a Compelling Patient Experience

Crafting an unforgettable patient experience revolves around genuine care and delivering extra value. Start by fostering a warm and welcoming atmosphere within your practice. Ensure that the physical environment is comfortable and that the staff is approachable and empathetic.

Invest time in understanding each patient's unique needs and concerns. Personalize interactions by addressing them by name and acknowledging their individuality. Demonstrate active listening during appointments, making patients feel heard and valued.

Go beyond the expected by providing educational resources, ensuring patients leave with a deeper understanding of their health. Implementing technology for efficient communication and appointment scheduling adds convenience and enhances the overall experience.

Create a seamless and empathetic journey, from the first point of contact to post-appointment follow-ups. Utilize feedback mechanisms to understand patient satisfaction and continuously improve services.

Consider offering small gestures of kindness, such as follow-up calls, wellness newsletters, or educational workshops. These extra touches demonstrate a commitment to holistic well-being and contribute to a lasting positive impression.

Ultimately, an exceptional patient experience is built on the foundation of genuine care, personalized attention, and the added value that goes beyond medical treatment. By consistently exceeding expectations, healthcare providers can create memorable experiences that foster trust, loyalty, and a sense of genuine connection with their patients.

Hidden Strategy No. 4: Create A Compelling Patient Experience (and keep them coming back for more!)

Create a Positive and Lasting First Impression

These are simple, low-cost strategies guaranteed to make someone feel welcomed.

Educate visiting prospective patients by using

- Videos of the procedure
- Videos of any training or talks you have given
- Digital photo frames showcasing your work

- Photo Album of before and after photos of the procedure they are interested in
- DVDs of you, your staff, your practice, and patient testimonials
- Forms to fill out ahead of time (complete them as much as possible for them before sending)
- A quality folder to hold the above materials

Ensure you have a testimonial album on the coffee table that includes

- Patient surveys
- Testimonials, Thank you cards, etc.
- PR efforts (media coverage)
- Articles you've written
- Skills & Expertise
- Speaking Engagements
- Special Awards
- Personal: Family and Hobbies

Make your patients feel special by personalizing their experience.

For example: Less Impersonal vs. More personal

- Rather than a newsletter >>> Personalized letter
- Rather than an email >>> A direct mail invitation
- Rather than a brochure >>> An interactive Website

- Less patient contact >>> More one to one time with patients

Show Consideration + Show Appreciation + Recognition is essential

- **The Key Point:** Better service means more engaged patients, spending more money, more frequently!
- **Focus on Attentiveness:** Ensure you and your team become “masters of detail.”

❍ ❍ ❍ ❍

CHAPTER 5

Easy Conversions: Decrease the Number of Patients You Lose

Boosting patient conversion is about better communication, personalized care, and smoother processes. Here are some simple strategies to get more patients on board:

1. **Responsive & Relatable Communication:**
    - Ensure prompt and relatable communication through various channels such as phone, email, and online messaging, tailored to patients' preferences.
    - Clearly communicate the benefits of your services, addressing patient concerns and questions comprehensively.
2. **User-Friendly Online Presence:**
    - Optimize your website for user-friendliness, making it easy for potential patients to find information and schedule appointments.
    - Implement online appointment scheduling and provide clear instructions for new patient onboarding.

3. **Patient Education:**
    - Develop educational materials or host workshops that empower patients with information about their health and your services.
    - Use multimedia formats to explain procedures, treatments, and preventive measures.
4. **Personalized Interactions:**
    - Tailor your approach to each patient, acknowledging their individual needs and preferences during consultations.
    - Utilize patient data to personalize communication, creating a more meaningful connection.
5. **Efficient Follow-Up Systems:**
    - Implement effective follow-up systems to check on patients after appointments.
    - Send post-visit surveys to gather feedback and identify areas for improvement.
6. **Streamlined Appointment Processes:**
    - Simplify appointment scheduling and registration processes to minimize friction.
    - Leverage technology for automated appointment reminders and easy check-ins.
7. **Transparent Pricing:**
    - Clearly communicate your pricing structure, insurance information, and any potential additional costs.
    - Offer transparent financial options and discounts where applicable.

8. **Referral Programs:**
   - Implement referral programs that incentivize existing patients to recommend your services to others.
   - Offer discounts or perks for successful referrals.

By combining these strategies, healthcare providers can create a patient-centric approach that not only attracts new patients but also fosters loyalty and satisfaction, ultimately leading to increased patient conversion.

Hidden Strategy No. 5: Decrease the Number of Patients You Lose!

Use the following proven tools to wake up your sleeping patients and get them returning and referring their friends:

- Internal laser-focused marketing
- Be smart about your internal communications: Start with your more mature, affluent patients
- If you haven't seen some patients for some time — send them a 'Welcome Back' card in the post
- Loyalty cards and referral cards work well
- The Key Point: Retention is the new patient acquisition

CHAPTER 6

Social Media: Mistakes to Avoid

Avoiding social media mistakes is crucial for maintaining a professional and trustworthy online presence for your medical practice. Here are common pitfalls to steer clear of:

1. **Violating Patient Privacy:** Avoid sharing any patient information, even in a de-identified form. Respect patient confidentiality and adhere strictly to privacy regulations.
2. **Misleading Information:** Provide accurate and reliable health information. Avoid making exaggerated claims or sharing misleading content that could harm patients or erode trust.
3. **Ignoring HIPAA (Health Insurance Portability and Accountability Act) Compliance:** Understand and adhere to HIPAA regulations when using social media. Ensure that all staff members are educated on the importance of patient privacy.
4. **Overlooking Professionalism:** Maintain a professional tone and demeanor in all social media interactions. Avoid engaging in online disputes or sharing inappropriate content.

5. **Ignoring Negative Feedback:** Respond to negative feedback in a constructive and empathetic manner. Ignoring or responding defensively can damage your reputation.
6. **Inconsistent Branding:** Maintain a consistent brand image across all social media platforms. Use a consistent logo, profile picture, and branding elements to enhance recognition.
7. **Ignoring Regular Updates:** Keep your social media profiles updated with accurate information, including office hours, contact details, and any changes in services or staff.
8. **Overlooking Engagement:** Engage with your audience by responding to comments and messages. Ignoring inquiries or feedback can create a negative perception of your practice.
9. **Neglecting a Social Media Policy:** Establish a social media policy for your staff to ensure that everyone understands the guidelines for representing the practice online.
10. **Excessive Self-Promotion:** Balance promotional content with valuable and informative posts. Constant self-promotion may deter followers. Share relevant healthcare news, tips, and educational content.
11. **Ignoring Analytics:** Regularly review social media analytics to understand what content resonates with your audience. Adjust your strategy based on insights to improve engagement.

By avoiding these social media mistakes and maintaining a thoughtful, professional, and patient-centric approach, your medical practice can harness the benefits of social media while mitigating potential risks.

CHAPTER 7

Increase Efficiency: Decrease the Running Cost of a Hospital or Nursing Home

ZERO TOLERANCE for waste, mistakes, sloppiness, indifference, stupidity, squandered leads, and lost patients because you didn't negotiate with suppliers.

You don't have to be slick to get what you want in a negotiation; just be well-prepared and have the time and interest to see and deal with it.

Step 1: Know Your Facts

- What is the fair market value of the property?
- Who is responsible for the utilities—such as electric, water/sewer, and telephones?
- Who is responsible for the maintenance fees?
- Who is responsible for the rates?
- What is the minimum term of the lease, and are there guaranteed renewal options?

- Is there a cancellation clause, and if so, what are the terms and conditions?
- Are there restrictions on hours of operation, including nights and weekends?
- What are the security deposits, and are there any non-refundable fees?
- Are you allowed to operate your type of business in this facility, and are there any competitors that might restrict you from doing business there?
- Register with your local council.
- Are you allowed to build or add to the facility, and do you have to restore it to its original condition upon your departure?

Step 2: Negotiate

The following are additional areas that should be part of your negotiation:

- Always ask to "test drive" the equipment. Ask the sales rep to bring the device to your facility so you can operate it and get a feel for it.
- Is the manufacturer's warranty adequate, or do you want to negotiate for an extension beyond the offered warranty?
- Can the warranty be transferred if you sell the equipment before the negotiated warranty expires? This can be sticky, but sometimes it can be negotiated into the deal.

- Is there a warranty or an extended warranty for parts or labour? Read the fine print carefully.
- Are the charges for delivery included in the upfront costs, or are they extra?
- Are you responsible for shipping costs when you have to send the equipment back for repair?
- Will you get a "loan" piece of equipment when your unit is out of service?
- Try to negotiate additional consumables in the deal.
- Ask the supplier to explain what finance is available and make sure you understand the differences between leasing and cash or bank loan purchasing.
- Remember whether to analyse how quickly your new piece of equipment will make money — make sure you only buy established, tried-and-tested INCOME GENERATORS with proven track records and marketing support.

Step 3:

Listen to your instincts and keep an eye on any red flags or warning signs that may arise during negotiations.

Step 4: Reduce the costs

- **The Key Points:** Here are some effective methods of reducing overheads and expenses:
  - If you accept credit cards, do your research to find out who may reduce their processing charges to get

your business. When you pay your bills, use your credit cards to receive points and airline miles.

- If you use only one company for all of your practice supplies, you are probably paying too much for some of your monthly supplies. Ask them for volume discounts or discounts if you pay within 30 days.
- You could also develop an inventory management system and reduce the amount of stock on your shelves (although it would not affect your practice or patient demand).
- You could also consider renegotiating your lease if you accept an extension and are then able to reduce your monthly rent. Remember, there are some towns and cities that will help by lowering your rates.
- Make sure you always avoid costly overtime and only allow authorised overtime.
- You can avoid using expensive temporary staff by cross-training your staff to fill in when your team is absent or sick.
- You can also introduce an 'Absence Management Policy' which helps to manage this process and ensures that everyone knows where they stand on sick pay and other entitlements.
- Use a great accountant.

❍ ❍ ❍ ❍

CHAPTER 8

Staff Training and Development: Building a High-Performing Team

The success of any medical organization hinges on the quality of care delivered, and this, in turn, is directly correlated to the competence and dedication of its staff. Continuous staff training and development are not mere luxuries but indispensable investments that can significantly elevate the overall performance of your practice.

The Significance of Staff Training and Development

A well-trained and motivated staff is the cornerstone of a thriving medical practice. Investing in their growth yields numerous benefits:

- **Enhanced Patient Care:** Up-to-date knowledge and skills lead to improved patient outcomes, satisfaction, and loyalty.

- **Increased Efficiency:** Skilled staff can streamline processes, reduce errors, and optimize resource utilization.
- **Boosted Morale:** Employees who feel valued and supported are more engaged and productive.
- **Improved Retention:** Opportunities for growth and development foster employee loyalty and reduce turnover.
- **Competitive Advantage:** A highly skilled team differentiates your practice from competitors.

Identifying Training Needs

Before implementing any training program, it's crucial to identify the specific skills and knowledge gaps within your team. Conduct regular performance reviews, gather employee feedback, and analyze patient satisfaction surveys to pinpoint areas for improvement.

Designing Effective Training Programs

Tailor your training programs to address identified needs. Consider the following approaches:

- **On-the-Job Training:** Provide hands-on experience under the guidance of experienced staff members.
- **Formal Classroom Training:** Offer structured learning sessions covering specific topics or skills.
- **Online Learning:** Utilize e-learning platforms for flexibility and accessibility.

- **Mentorship and Coaching:** Pair employees with experienced mentors for personalized guidance.

Fostering a Culture of Continuous Learning

Create a workplace culture that prioritizes learning and development:

- **Encourage Skill Development:** Support employees in pursuing certifications, licenses, or advanced degrees.
- **Provide Opportunities for Growth:** Offer career paths and promotion opportunities within the practice.
- **Recognize and Reward Learning:** Celebrate employee achievements and milestones.
- **Lead by Example:** Demonstrate a commitment to lifelong learning as a practice leader.

Building a High-Performing Team

Effective training is essential, but it's equally important to cultivate a positive work environment that fosters teamwork and collaboration:

- **Clear Communication:** Establish open and transparent communication channels.
- **Shared Goals:** Clearly define team objectives and ensure everyone understands their role.
- **Empowerment:** Delegate authority and encourage employee input.
- **Recognition and Appreciation:** Acknowledge and reward team contributions.

- **Conflict Resolution:** Implement strategies for addressing and resolving conflicts.
- **Team Building Activities:** Organize team-building events to strengthen relationships.

By investing in your staff's growth and creating a supportive work environment, you can build a high-performing team that drives the success of your medical practice. Remember, training and development are ongoing processes that require continuous evaluation and adaptation to meet the evolving needs of your practice and patients.

❍ ❍ ❍ ❍

CHAPTER 9

Legal and Ethical Considerations

The healthcare industry is heavily regulated, and medical practices must navigate a complex landscape of laws and ethical guidelines. Adherence to these standards is not just a legal requirement but also essential for building trust with patients and maintaining a strong reputation.

Patient Confidentiality

Patient confidentiality is a cornerstone of the medical profession. Protecting patient information is crucial to maintaining trust and complying with regulations such as HIPAA (Health Insurance Portability and Accountability Act) in the United States. Key considerations include:

- **Data Security:** Implementing robust security measures to safeguard electronic and paper records.
- **Access Control:** Limiting access to patient information to authorized personnel.
- **Patient Education:** Informing patients about their privacy rights and how their information is protected.

Informed Consent

Obtaining informed consent is a fundamental ethical and legal obligation. Patients have the right to understand their medical conditions, treatment options, potential risks, and benefits before making decisions. Essential elements of informed consent include:

- **Clear Communication:** Explaining medical information in understandable terms.
- **Disclosure of Information:** Providing comprehensive information about treatment options, including alternatives and potential risks.
- **Patient Comprehension:** Ensuring patients understand the information presented.
- **Voluntary Consent:** Obtaining written and verbal consent from patients.

Regulatory Compliance

Staying up-to-date with ever-changing regulations is essential for avoiding legal and financial penalties. Key areas of compliance include:

- **Licensing and Certification:** Maintaining required licenses and certifications for staff and the practice.
- **Medicare and Medicaid:** Understanding and complying with billing and reimbursement regulations.
- **HIPAA:** Implementing and maintaining HIPAA compliance to protect patient information.

- **State and Local Laws:** Adhering to specific state and local regulations related to healthcare.

Ethical Decision Making

Ethical dilemmas often arise in healthcare. A strong ethical framework can guide decision-making and protect the interests of patients and the practice. Key principles include:

- **Patient Autonomy:** Respecting patients' rights to make decisions about their own healthcare.
- **Beneficence:** Acting in the best interests of patients.
- **Non-maleficence:** Avoiding harm to patients.
- **Justice:** Treating patients fairly and equitably.

Creating a Culture of Compliance

A culture of compliance starts at the top. Leaders must demonstrate a commitment to ethical behavior and compliance. Key strategies include:

- **Regular Training:** Providing ongoing training on legal and ethical issues.
- **Open Communication:** Encouraging staff to report concerns or potential violations.
- **Risk Assessment:** Identifying and mitigating potential risks to patient safety and compliance.
- **Documentation:** Maintaining accurate and complete records.

By prioritizing legal and ethical considerations, medical practices can protect patients, mitigate risks, and build a strong foundation for success.

❍ ❍ ❍ ❍

CHAPTER 10

Innovations in Patient Engagement

The healthcare landscape is undergoing a digital transformation, with technology playing an increasingly pivotal role in patient care. One of the most significant areas of innovation is patient engagement. By leveraging mobile apps and wearable technology, healthcare providers can enhance patient experience, improve adherence to treatment plans, and ultimately, deliver better health outcomes.

The Power of Mobile Apps

Mobile apps offer a convenient and accessible platform for patients to manage their health. They can be used to:

- **Enhanced Communication:** Mobile apps enable real-time communication between patients and healthcare providers. Features like instant messaging, video consultations, and appointment scheduling make it easier for patients to seek advice, report symptoms, and receive timely feedback.

- **Personalized Health Management:** Apps can offer personalized health management plans based on individual patient data. This includes medication reminders, dietary suggestions, and exercise routines tailored to the patient's specific needs and conditions.
- **Educational Resources:** Many apps provide access to a wealth of educational resources, including articles, videos, and tutorials. This empowers patients with the knowledge they need to manage their health more effectively.
- **Remote Monitoring:** Mobile apps can be integrated with wearable devices to monitor vital signs and health metrics remotely. This allows healthcare providers to track patient health in real-time and intervene promptly if any abnormalities are detected.
- **Data Tracking and Analysis:** Apps enable patients to log and track their health data, such as blood pressure, glucose levels, and physical activity. This data can be shared with healthcare providers for more informed decision-making and personalized care plans.

The Impact of Wearable Technology

Wearable technology, including smartwatches, fitness trackers, and medical devices, have the potential to revolutionize patient care by providing real-time data on vital signs and physical activity. These devices can help in:

- **Continuous Health Monitoring:** Wearable devices can continuously monitor vital signs such as heart rate, blood pressure, and oxygen levels. This continuous monitoring provides a comprehensive picture of the patient's health, enabling early detection of potential issues.
- **Improved Adherence to Treatment Plans:** Wearables can send reminders for medication, exercise, and other aspects of a treatment plan. This helps patients adhere to their prescribed regimen, improving health outcomes.
- **Motivation and Engagement:** Wearables often include features like goal setting, progress tracking, and gamification to motivate patients to stay active and engaged in their health management.
- **Emergency Alerts:** Some wearable devices are equipped with emergency alert systems that can notify healthcare providers or family members if the patient experiences a medical emergency, such as a fall or a sudden drop in vital signs.
- **Data Integration:** Wearables can sync with mobile apps and electronic health records (EHRs), ensuring that all health data is consolidated in one place. This integration facilitates better communication and coordination between patients and healthcare providers.

Real-World Applications and Success Stories

Several real-world applications and success stories illustrate the impact of mobile apps and wearable technology on patient engagement:

- **Chronic Disease Management:** Apps like MySugr for diabetes management and Omada Health for chronic disease prevention offer personalized coaching, progress tracking, and educational resources, helping patients manage their conditions effectively.
- **Post-Surgery Recovery:** Apps like SeamlessMD guide patients through their post-surgery recovery process, providing step-by-step instructions, reminders, and progress tracking. This results in improved recovery rates and reduced readmission rates.
- **Mental Health Support:** Wearables and apps like Headspace and Calm offer guided meditation, stress management techniques, and mental health tracking, helping users maintain their mental well-being.
- **Cardiac Monitoring:** Devices like the Apple Watch and Fitbit can detect irregular heart rhythms and alert users to potential cardiac issues, prompting timely medical intervention.

By embracing the opportunities offered by mobile apps and wearable technology, healthcare providers can transform the way they interact with patients and improve overall health outcomes.

In the words of healthcare futurist Bertalan Meskó, "The future of medicine lies in connected patients, wearable technology, and artificial intelligence."

And Because I Care for You...

And aim to improve India's healthcare system for both providers and patients, I am adding some bonus (checklists) that will be highly beneficial for you...

"Healing happens when hearts and expertise connect."

-Deepti Gupta

BONUS #1

Build Your Dream Team

The Right Staff Is Critical to Your Success.

Most aesthetic practitioners face challenges with their staff:

- Their staff does not care about their practice like they do.
- Their staff is not converting prospective patients into paying patients. (In fact, often they chase patients away.)
- Their staff does not know how to promote the practitioner as the best choice for patients.

So, do you have the right team in place?

If you're not sure whether you're surrounded by team players, hold a friendly staff referral competition.

You know the team members you do wish to have on board.

The whole team should acknowledge and understand just how important the front desk position is. They are usually receiving the lowest pay but the highest amount of pressure.

Do you know why your employees leave?

Here are the most common reasons why your staff may move on:

- Lack of recognition and appreciation (a huge one)
- Lack of leadership from the management
- Lack of understanding of their role
- Not feeling part of the team
- Not getting along with other staff
- They lack clear job descriptions
- Work is not meaningful
- They feel as though they are not contributing
- Feeling stressed and overworked
- Higher salaries and benefits
- There is no career path or training plan

The Key Point: Finding good people is only half the battle. The other half is retaining them. And you can achieve that by:

- Staff Lunch Meetings
- Work as a Team — Celebrate as a Team
- Friendly Staff Competitions
- Cross-Training all staff to cover sickness and absenteeism
- BONUS - Increase your number of new patients (without breaking the bank)

❍ ❍ ❍ ❍

BONUS #2

Increase the Number of New Patients (Without Breaking the Bank!)

Marketing is all about education. The goal is to get prospective patients to raise their hands to say they are interested. Maybe not now, or not yet, but one day when they are ready. You only have one chance to make the first impression.

How to convert a phone enquiry into a booking for a consultation:

- Have a positive attitude
- Make sure there is a friendly greeting and you ask who is calling
- Bond by asking questions
- Attach emotion to the problem and solution
- Qualify them, so you know where they are in the process (It's all about "when" they are booking, not "if" they are booking.)
- Close appointment with a question

- Get contact information and book an appointment (Send a Welcome Package. The package should include all or most of the following):
    - Welcome letter with handwritten comments
    - Description of the consultation process so they expect to spend time with you, your staff and your office (the more time they spend with you, the more perceived value)
    - Info on procedures they are interested in
    - Patient testimonials in story-form
    - Before/after photos with good results
    - Practice Brochure
    - Meet the doctor: - Career highlights
- **Overcoming Objections**
    - Repeat back and respond
    - Nudge using questions and attempt close again
    - Negotiate and attempt close again

Why Is It Important to Have a Short- and Long-Term Marketing Strategy?

- **Use your marketing strategy to achieve the following:**
    - Bring in new patients
    - Increase sales (from existing patients)
    - Improve patient loyalty and get existing patients to buy more
    - Introduce a new treatment or service
    - Increase your market share in your local area(s)
    - Establish and build your brand

- Launch an advertising campaign
- Launch a PR campaign
- Encourage word of mouth referrals and recommendations
- Retain existing profitable patients (i.e., those that buy more than one treatment)
- Make patients feel more valued (by providing value-added service)
- Offer existing patients exclusive offers
- Ensure your business continually evolves and remains innovative, fresh, and new

Market analysis involves studying the market conditions, trends, and factors that impact your industry, like who your customers are and what they want. **Competitor analysis** means looking at your rivals to see what they're doing well and where they could improve. **Company analysis** includes figuring out what makes your business unique, what benefits it offers to customers, how you communicate that to them, what your goals are, and how you measure success. INSTEAD OF DISCOUNTING, YOU RAISE YOUR PRICES.

Doing this can help you in many ways:

- **Better Positioning:** Higher prices can make your brand look more exclusive and special compared to others.
- **Higher Perceived Value:** People might think your products or services are better just because they cost more.

➢ **Higher Quality Buyers:** Raising prices can attract customers who are willing to pay more for better quality, which can make your business more successful in the long run.

❍ ❍ ❍ ❍

BONUS #3

Enhance Online Presence

Website Optimization

- Conduct thorough keyword research to identify relevant terms.
- Optimize website title tags, meta descriptions, and header tags.
- Improve website loading speed.
- Create high-quality, informative content.
- Ensure mobile-friendliness of the website.

Social Media Management

- Identify the target audience and select appropriate platforms.
- Develop a consistent posting schedule.
- Share valuable content, including blog posts, patient testimonials, and practice news.
- Engage with followers through comments and messages.
- Use relevant hashtags to increase visibility.

Online Reputation Management

- Monitor online reviews regularly.
- Respond promptly and professionally to all reviews.
- Encourage satisfied patients to leave reviews.
- Address negative reviews privately and publicly.
- Utilize online reputation management tools if necessary.

Content Creation

- Develop a content calendar to plan posts.
- Create engaging blog posts, articles, and videos.
- Share patient stories and success stories.
- Optimize content for search engines.
- Promote content through social media and email marketing.

BONUS #4

Streamline Operations

Scheduling and Appointment Management

- Implement a patient-friendly online appointment booking system.
- Optimize appointment scheduling to minimize patient wait times and maximize provider productivity.
- Utilize appointment reminders to reduce no-shows.

Inventory Management

- Conduct regular inventory audits to identify overstocked or understocked items.
- Implement a system for tracking inventory usage and expiration dates.
- Explore automated inventory management solutions.
- Optimize ordering processes to reduce stockouts.

Administrative Efficiency

- Digitize patient records and implement electronic health records (EHR).

- Automate routine tasks like appointment reminders and billing.
- Streamline patient registration and check-in processes.
- Implement a centralized communication system.
- Delegate tasks to appropriate staff members.
- Regularly review and update office policies and procedures.
- Explore cloud-based solutions for data storage and backup.
- Implement a document management system.
- Utilize practice management software to integrate various aspects of operations.

❍ ❍ ❍ ❍

BONUS #5

Enhancing Patient Safety

Staff Training and Development

- Conduct regular patient safety training for all staff.
- Implement mandatory continuing education programs.
- Provide training on medication administration and error prevention.
- Offer training on fire safety and emergency procedures.
- Emphasize the importance of effective communication among staff.

Safety Protocols

- Develop and implement clear patient identification procedures.
- Establish protocols for preventing falls and injuries.
- Create guidelines for handling and disposing of hazardous materials.
- Implement infection prevention and control measures.
- Develop a system for reporting and analyzing adverse events.

Safety Audits and Assessments

- Conduct regular safety audits of the practice.
- Review and update emergency preparedness plans.
- Assess the effectiveness of safety protocols.
- Identify and address potential safety hazards.
- Implement a system for tracking and reporting safety incidents.

❍ ❍ ❍ ❍

Your Practice, Your Prosperity

Attention Medical Practitioners!

Ready to elevate your practice? Take your medical journey to new heights with insights from this book to attract more patients and grow your business.

Looking for expert advice? I'm ready to guide you!

I'm here for you! Reach out via

gargdee@gmail.com

or

WhatsApp/Contact me at ***9811849847*** to explore how we can maximize your practice's potential together.

Let's make your practice thrive!